Abortion funds: The story of Olivia Julianna abortion fund raiser

Laura L. Shilling

Table of contents

Chapter one

Abortion funds

What are abortion funds?

An early termination store is a philanthropic association that gives direct financing to those looking for a fetus removal who will be unable to manage the cost of it.

A few assets totally or to some degree cover the costs stringently connected with the method, for example, for pills for drug fetus removals - - which make up the greater part of all early terminations in the U.S. - - or for an in-office system.

"We additionally give what we call reasonable help," Chasity Wilson, leader head of the New Orleans Abortion Fund, which gives financing to individuals living in the Gulf South, told ABC News.

This encompasses expenses, for example, transportation to and from early termination centers, interpretation administrations, gas, housing, kid care - - and everyday encouragement.

Notwithstanding neighborhood assets, there are 92 fetus removal reserves - - as of October 2021 - - that are individuals from the National Network of Abortion Funds, which interfaces with associations of the nation over.

Fetus removal reserves offer help to pregnant individuals looking for early termination. Early termination can cost up to $750 in the main trimester, and up to $1,500 later in pregnancy, as per Planned Parenthood. What's more, a few states have limited Medicaid, confidential plans, and Affordable Care Act commercial center plans from covering early termination.

Such assets have been a critical device for fetus removal freedoms advocates over the most recent quite a while. As Republican legislators have sanctioned neighborhood regulations to limit fetus removal in their states, early termination has become unavailable to a large number of patients, especially BIPOC individuals, low-pay individuals, and those living in country regions.

A close all-out fetus removal boycott in Texas, for example, put 7 million ladies of contraceptive age something like 247 miles from open early termination care. (That is multiple times the distance they would have needed to go before the boycott came full circle.)

Early termination subsidizes pay for the medical services and additionally travel expenses a few patients will most likely be unable to manage.

Who donates to abortion funds?

Most early termination reserves are upheld by individual gifts. What's more, a surge of new gifts has come over the most recent a little while. The National Network of Abortion Funds (NNAF) — which, as of October 2020, included

92 fetus removal reserves — told Good Morning America that it got more than $1.5 million in gifts in the three days after Politico distributed a spilled draft of the Dobbs choice on May 2.

Such countless individuals attempted to cause their site to crash. On June 24, when the Supreme Court gave over its choice, their site abortionfunds.org seemed to have again crashed.

The gift flood is genuinely necessary, as per advocates. The NNAF says that most fetus removal assets can oblige somewhere close to one-quarter and 33% of guests who request their help with paying for early termination and its related costs like travel and childcare (which can be basic because most ladies who look for fetus removals are as of now moms).

A delegate for Fund Texas Choice, which takes care of Texans' movement expenses to out-of-state fetus removal facilities, told CBS in May, before Roe was canceled, that the association previously was handling more than 300 calls per month. It had the assets to help just 130 patients, every one of whom required $750 to $1,000 in help. They expected much more calls after Roe was struck down. Early termination freedoms advocates noticed that movement costs have as of late been exacerbated by high gas costs.

What precisely do abortion funds pay for?

Each asset works suddenly. Some totally or somewhat cover the costs that are completely connected with the actual strategy, similar to pills for clinical fetus removals — which make up the greater part of all early terminations in the United States — or an in-office technique.

While those looking for fetus removals are deferred in their arrangements by center limit, lawful limitations, and the need to assemble cash for the technique, they are frequently pushed later into pregnancy, and the end turns out to be more costly the later a pregnant individual pauses. Different assets help pay for personal expenses related to going out of state for early termination, similar to transportation, gas, housing, and food.

They additionally can offer different types of assistance like interpretation, organizing and paying for childcare, and giving everyday encouragement.

Numerous fetus removal reserves are more unambiguous in their concentration, whether that center is geographic (like the Midwest Access Coalition), social (like Indigenous Women Rising), or strategic (like the Brigid Alliance, which assists pay for those patients who with heading out significant distances to get early terminations later in pregnancy).

How, precisely, an asset interfaces with and supports patients looking for care for monetary help relies upon their particular strategies. Certain nearby subsidies will give funds straightforwardly to ladies who contact the association, while reserves like the Women's Reproductive Rights Assistance Project request that facilities and suppliers charge them straightforwardly.

Changes in state regulations might affect these singular assets. The Texas Equal Access Fund declared Friday that they are stopping subsidizing: "Because of the vulnerability and hazard of what the choice could bring, we are stopping financing today until we have gotten an opportunity to comprehend the choice whenever it is delivered," the association tweeted. They guided expected patients to the site Ineedana.com, a public facility catalog.

"We are incensed," tweeted the Jane Fund, a Massachusetts-based fetus removal reserve. Yet, the association guaranteed supporters that they and other early termination reserves "will keep on doing what we excel at — store fetus removals."

Chapter Two

How abortion funds work

A few patients might need to pay more than $1,000 to get an early termination

What's next for early termination privileges in America?

A spilled draft assessment demonstrates the Supreme Court could decide for a Mississippi regulation and topple Roe v. Swim before long, prompting a far-reaching update of fetus removal rights. As a developing number of states keep on passing severe early termination regulations, Americans are confronting more hindrances with regards to getting to the methodology.

Be that as it may, perhaps of the best hindrance pregnant individuals are frequently met with is the expense of acquiring an early termination.

A fetus removal can cost somewhere in the range of $0 to more than $1,000, and it's not only the clinical costs that patients face, as per a review from the Guttmacher Institute, an exploration bunch zeroing in on sexual and conceptive wellbeing.

Those looking for the early termination may likewise have personal expenses for going away - - or, at times, out of state - - as well as food, dwelling, gas, planning youngster care, and getting to prescription.

Presently, with the Supreme Court possibly set to upset or seriously stomach Roe v. Swim, consideration has gone to early termination reserves, which can help orchestrate and pay for fetus removal care, as well as different expenses related to the method.

A few assets, like the NOAF, permit ladies to call straightforwardly to request help paying for early termination.

"The patient connects by calling our hotlines," Wilson said. "At times we likewise partake in fortitude assets when another asset that offers these types of assistance might connect and say, 'Hello, we have an individual whose techniques cost $1,300 so we can burn through $500, what amount could you at any point help?'"

Different assets, for example, the Women's Reproductive Rights Assistance Project - - a charity that gives assets to individuals looking for early termination administrations or crisis contraception - - talk straightforwardly with facilities and suppliers.

"We have an organization of more than 700 facilities, specialists and medical clinics that are connected with our asset that reach us consistently to tell us that they have a patent needing a fetus removal and that patient requirements subsidizing," Sylvia Ghazarian, leader overseer of WRRAP, told ABC News. "At the point when a center calls us, we return the call and make a vow obligation to that facility."

WRRAP's measurements from 2021 showed that 73% of the asset's patients were ethnic minorities and 76% got public help. Moreover,

NOAF's 2021 report viewed that 71% of patients were Black or African American and around 66% were on Medicaid.

"A ton of these populaces have customarily less admittance to medical services, yet in no way, shape or form does this mean these are the populaces that get early terminations most often," Wilson said.

Who can get to them?

Some fetus removal reserves have no prerequisites. Ghazarian said WRRAP gives subsidizing to fetus removals across the U.S.

Different assets help explicit gatherings of ladies in light of where they reside, their racial/ethnic cosmetics, or how far along they are in their pregnancies.

For instance, the Midwest Access Coalition helps cover costs for individuals looking for early terminations in the Midwest, while the Northwest Abortion Access Fund does likewise for those living in Alaska, Idaho, Oregon, and Washington.

Others, similar to the Brigid Alliance, assist with financing the individuals who need to venture out significant distances to get late-term fetus removals.

Chapter Three

Olivia Julianna abortion fundraiser

An Abortion rights extremist Olivia Julianna, a Teen who was as of late body disgraced by Matt Gaetz has Raised Over $700,000 For Abortion Funds.

"I'm extremely excited that I've been able to use my platform to do something that will genuinely make a tangible difference in people's lives."

In the fantasy, Rumpelstiltskin can transform straw into gold. In Texas, a gathering of understudy activists and tacticians called Gen-Z For Change transformed a profoundly private affront into medical services. In the wake of being "body-disgraced" by Congressman Matt Gaetz on Twitter, 19-year-old Olivia Julianna raised more than $711,000 for early termination finances all through the nation, zeroing in on states hardest hit by post-Roe limitations. As of press time, quite possibly her latest tweet says thanks to Gaetz for "making a difference" in her endeavors, adding "Matt, I'd love to send you a bouquet of flowers. I'll send one for every hundred thousand dollars we raise."

This story started on July 24 at the Turning Point USA Student Action Summit in Tampa, a social event for extreme right youth. In a discourse, Gaetz, a Republican senator from Florida, directed his concentration toward fetus removal privileges activists. "Can anyone explain why the ladies with minimal probability of getting pregnant are the ones most stressed over having fetus removals? No one needs to impregnate you in the event that you seem to be a thumb!" he declared to dissipated chuckling and good wishes. "These individuals are accursed from the back to front. They're similar to 5' 2", 350 pounds, and they're like, 'Give me my fetus removals or I'll get up and walk and dissent!" (Later, Gaetz multiplied down on his remarks, telling WEAR ABC3 that he was for sure calling protestors "revolting and overweight" and that they ought to "be irritated," in this way turning "Be Offended" into a Twitter image.)

Julianna took to Twitter also to voice her hatred for Gaetz's assertions, saying "It has become obvious that Matt Gaetz — claimed pedophile — has said that it's dependably the 'terrible... 5'2" 350-pound" ladies that 'no one needs to impregnate' who rally for early termination. I'm really 5'11". 6'4" in heels. I wear them so the little men like you are helped to remember your place."

Hours after the fact, the senator, who was not labeled in Julianna's tweet, retweeted a Newsmax article with the title "Florida Rep. Matt Gaetz impacted early termination activists in a tirade sure to raise the dander of his political rivals" in which he shared a screen capture of Julianna's profile picture with the going with the text "Dander raised."

Julianna strikes back.

In the unfading expressions of Vivian Ward: serious mix-up. Large. Tremendous. Julianna's virtual entertainment barrage was quick.

"Think about what, Matty," she snickered on TikTok, "I'm not the one."

She spent the remainder of July 24 posting a progression of images and jokes without regard to Gaetz prior to settling on a more substantial game-plan by means of Gen-Z For Change, a charitable association where she is a tactician.

Julianna started an early termination reserve on July 25.

"To pay tribute to Matt Gaetz openly body disgracing me, I'll raise support for the @genzforchange early termination reserve," she declared.

In the days since the mission was sent off, Julianna has gotten an overflow of media inclusion and, as per her, own help from across various web-based entertainment stages. The Gen-Z for the Choice asset has raised more than $711,000 and then some. To give a thought to how rapidly that number is rising, when we started revealing this story that number had just barely passed the $600,000 boundary.

Julianna repeated in a meeting with Joy-Ann Reid that the cash is being parted among 50 fetus removal reserves ", particularly in states where those administrations will be required the most on account of prohibitive early termination regulations."

"I'm very energized that I've had the option to utilize my foundation to accomplish something that will really have a substantial effect on individuals' lives," she said.

Julianna has spent a lot of her online entertainment energy throughout the last week featuring her raising support endeavors. While she has been dependent upon analysis and extra affronts from the right, she bats it away easily. "I'm a 19-year-old eccentric Latina — and that is the reason these lawmakers dread me," she tweeted. "Matt Gaetz and different conservatives are coming at coordinators with these infantile assaults since they realize ladies the nation over are assembling."

Eventually, Julianna accepts Gaetz's endeavored affront was a net decent. She even posted a picture of a card expressing gratitude toward him.

"Although your intentions were hateful, your public shaming of my appearance has done nothing but benefit me. I have gained a substantial amount of support across platforms, and now because of YOUR HATRED, I've also helped facilitate ... donations to abortion funds. Your hateful comments towards me will quite literally help pay for abortion services. LOL. Get rekt."

Chapter four

Impact of abortion funds

Brittany Mostiller, previous chief head of the Chicago Abortion Fund, said the asset's monetary help kept her from making more exceptional moves she'd thought about when she figured out she was pregnant.

Kim Floren has gone through the most recent a little while attempting to comfort individuals overreacting about the finish of Roe v. Swim.

"Everyone has been on the range from simply being in tears to add up to overreacting about the thing they will do," said Floren, who runs South Dakota's Justice Through Empowerment Network, one of in excess of 100 free early terminations subsidizes around the country.

Early termination subsidizes collection and appropriate cash to individuals who need assistance paying for fetus removals, including system and travel costs. In 2020, assets the nation over assisted almost 45,000 individuals with paying for fetus removals.

Most supports serve explicit states or locales, while others center around specific populaces like Indigenous ladies. Some, similar to Floren's, are run completely by volunteers. Others are essential for centers or bigger associations like Planned Parenthood.

Some early termination reserves have been around for quite a long time, however, their significance to fetus removal access is filling in a post-Roe world, particularly in states like South Dakota that currently boycott early termination.

"They will be truly indispensable for individuals to get to legitimate early termination out of state," said Gretchen Ely, a teacher of social work at the University of Tennessee and one of the country's couples of fetus removal store specialists.

Ely's examination has shown that early termination reserves principally serve individuals in their 20s who as of now have children and frequently need regular work, stable lodging, and safe connections. She additionally found that about a portion of early termination reserve clients is Black, contrasted with around 33% of in general fetus removal searchers.

"They serve individuals who have the best requirements," Ely said.

Early termination reserves give more than cash Brittany Mostiller originally found out about early termination assets in 2007.

She was 23 years of age and shared a two-room condo on the South Side of Chicago with her three children, her sister, and her niece. She had quite recently conveyed an impromptu pregnancy to term in February, which she said drove her into a downturn. Things deteriorated in July when she figured out she was pregnant once more.

"All that just felt like it was collapsing," she said of her life at that point. "I felt stuck. I needed something else. I needed to offer my kids something else."

Mostiller needed more cash for a fetus removal, which can cost anyplace from a couple hundred to two or three thousand bucks, contingent upon where you live and how far along the pregnancy is. At that point, Illinois' Medicaid program didn't cover fetus removals, something actually obvious in 34 states and Washington D.C.

The finish of Roe v. Swim has gigantic financial ramifications for male accomplices, as well

Mostiller connected with the not-for-profit Chicago Abortion Fund, which had the option to cover around 33% of what turned out to be a $900 early termination. They sent the cash straightforwardly to Mostiller's center. Fetus removal reserves frequently pay for just a piece of a client's early termination, in order to extend their restricted dollars to help whatever a number of individuals could be expected under the circumstances.

Mostiller said the monetary help from the fetus removal store kept her from making more exceptional moves she'd considered — like hurling herself down the steps or having her 5-year-old girl jump on her stomach to compel a premature delivery. In any case, she said the asset gave her significantly more than cash.

"I felt truly hung on that call and found such that I had never at any point felt," she said. "It gave me trust. [Things were] unpleasant, and they resembled this light."

Mostiller began chipping in with the Chicago Abortion Fund, and by 2015, she was its chief. She presently fills in as the authority improvement organizer at the National Network of Abortion Funds.

She said reserves have been planning for the fall of Roe since Donald Trump was chosen president a long time back.

"It's simply genuine now," she said. "They need all the help they can get."

More cash, more need
In the initial three weeks after the Supreme Court upset Roe v. Swim, the National Network of Abortion Funds raised almost $11 million for nearby assets, more than all early termination subsidies in the organization circulated in 2020.

Be that as it may, the request is likewise rising, expressed Floren of the South Dakota store. She said she got almost as many bring in the main seven-day stretch of July as she did in all of April, including a few from individuals beyond South Dakota frantic to find any individual who could help.

Guests are requesting more cash as well, as indicated by Floren. Fewer centers doing early terminations implies longer postponements, which can drive up a methodology's expense. What's more, since everybody in South Dakota needs to pass on the state to get a fetus removal, travel costs (known as "pragmatic help") are additionally going up.

Indeed, even before the Dobbs administration, more Americans were going for fetus removals

Indeed, even before the Dobbs administration, more Americans were going for early terminations
"When you include in someone who needs to travel 600 miles and afterward stay a few evenings in an inn, and afterward they need to eat that entire time while they're there ... a ton of times the pragmatic help costs similarly as much as the real financing for the early termination," Floren said.

Floren gauges she's now given out no less than $5,000 in functional help since a draft of the Supreme Court choice spilled in May. That is more than she spent on movement costs generally the year before. She consistently connects with other fetus removal assets to attempt to cobble together sufficient financing for guests.

"You simply attempt to make it somewhat more straightforward [for callers] on the grounds that it's now so troublesome," she said.

Unprecedented dread and vulnerability
Floren and other fetus removal store pioneers say the greatest change they've seen post-Roe is the manner by which terrified and uncertain individuals who call them are.

"I've had individuals come dependent upon me and say, 'I'm hesitant to call you all since I don't need my line getting tapped. I would rather not go to prison. I would rather not be captured,'" said Erin Smith, leader overseer of the Kentucky Health Justice Network.

While their asset serves all Kentuckians, the association centers, particularly around transsexual and nonbinary individuals who are in many cases avoided with regard to the early termination discussion. Smith expressed that working with these underestimated patients has set them up for the greater job they cnd up in post-Roe.

A drifting fetus removal facility is in the arranging stage, and individuals are now ready

"We are an enormous data center," Smith said. "Ensuring that in addition to the fact that we calling are our guests and consoling our guests, [but] that we're consoling the local area, that we're telling the local area what we should or shouldn't do or what they may or may not be able to."

Reserves are managing their own apprehension and vulnerability as well. Texas reserves have briefly quit paying for early terminations, uncertain on the off chance that they can legitimately work under the state's prohibitive regulations. Without a doubt, another asset in Alabama has done likewise. The National Network of Abortion Funds is offering awards to assist assets with recruiting legal advisors.

It's simply something more to stress over for reserves that were at that point battling to satisfy needs before Roe was upset. Study information from the National Network of Abortion Funds shows about a portion of individuals who call fetus removal reserves get no monetary help. Reserve pioneers are worried that gifts will slow while request remains high.

"I simply feel like it will deteriorate before it improves," Floren said. "Also, I don't think anyone truly understands what that will resemble. Also, that is the terrifying part."